To Zoe

SAINT PAUL

CTS Children's Books

With lots of love from
Nana xxx
31/3/19

Contents

Text by Silvia Vecchini
Illustrations by Antonio Vincenti
Translated by Simone Finaldi

Saint Paul: Published 2009 by the Incorporated Catholic Truth Society, 40-46 Harleyford Road, London SE11 5AY. Tel: 020 7640 0042; Fax: 020 7640 0046; www.CTSbooks.org. Copyright © 2009 The Incorporated Catholic Truth Society in this English-language edition.

ISBN: 978 1 86082 593 4   CTS Code CH 22

Translated from the original Italian Edition: **San Paolo** - ISBN 978-88-6124-087-2, published by Il Pozzo di Giacobbe, Corso Vittorio Emanuele 32/34, 91100 Trapani (TP), Italy © 2008 Crispino di Girolamo.

THE APOSTLE TO THE GENTILES

Paul did not know Jesus personally and was not one of the twelve. All the same, he is sometimes called "The thirteenth apostle". He is known as "the apostle to the gentiles" that is, the one who brought the Gospel to people who were not Jews. Paul was certainly the greatest missionary of all time. With his faith in the risen Christ, his energy, the witness of his life, his travels and his writings, he brought the Good News throughout the Mediterranean world of his time. He spread the message of Jesus: that salvation was for everyone.

THE YOUNG SAUL

Paul was born sometime between 8 and 12 BC. He lived and grew up with his family in Tarsus in Cilicia, which is in western Turkey. In the 1st century BC, Tarsus was a town on the border between East and West, there were plenty of Greeks, Romans and Anatolians in the port town, as well as a Jewish community. Paul's family, of the tribe of Benjamin, were part of that community, and like all the Jews of the time, he had two names, a Hebrew one "Saul", and a Latin and Greek name, "Paulus." Paul was a Jew but he was also a Roman citizen, like all the people of the city.

This was a privilege given to Tarsus because the people had supported Julius Caesar. Paul's father was a tent merchant and so Paul learnt to be a tent maker, a job that was useful to him on many occasions.

As a young man Paul went to school, he learnt Greek and was taught about the Greek culture of the time, then at a very young age he was sent to Jerusalem to receive a traditional Jewish education. His teacher was Gamaliel, the wisest and most famous Rabbi in the city. Very soon he knew the Law of Moses perfectly, as well as the oral traditions of his people, and he observed all the Law, as the other Pharisees did.

STANDING
BEFORE STEPHEN

When Paul finished studying he returned to Tarsus, and perhaps this is why he never met Christ when he was preaching. He only went back to Jerusalem after ten years or so.

When the young Paul came back to Jerusalem, he met the Christians. He heard that they were a dangerous sect threatening the Jews and their traditions.

In the year 36, a young deacon from the first Christian community was put on trial. Paul agreed with those who wanted to get rid of the Christians and stop them preaching. They condemned Stephen to death and stoned him, while Paul watched. He was still young, so the men of Jerusalem left him in charge of their cloaks while they killed Stephen.

6

Paul was known as a zealous Pharisee, proud of his origins and ready to do anything to defend the faith of his fathers. That is why he was given the task of finding and arresting Christians during the first persecution in Jerusalem.

Paul followed these orders, and, as he himself said, had many women and men who were disciples of Christ put in prison. One day, the council of the elders of the Jewish people gave him a letter to bring to the synagogue in Damascus. He was meant to arrest Christians and bring them back to Jerusalem, but something was about to change.

ON THE ROAD TO DAMASCUS

When he got near enough to the city to see the walls, Paul was suddenly blinded by a light. He fell, overcome by the vision, and while he was still wondering what was happening he heard a voice asking him, "Saul, Saul, why are you persecuting me?"

The men travelling with him heard the voice but could see nothing and they were afraid.

Paul understood the voice was really speaking to him. He fearfully asked, "Who are you Lord?"

The voice answered, "I am Jesus, whom you are persecuting!"

The voice had said "Jesus", the teacher of the people Paul was looking for. In that vision, Jesus had told Paul that to persecute his disciples was the same as persecuting him.

While he kept his hands over his eyes to protect them, the voice continued and told him, "Now, get up and go into the city. There, you will be told what to do!"

Paul tried to stand and opened his eyes to look about him, but he could see nothing. Those on the road with him saw that he was in difficulty and helped him make his way into the city.

A NEW LIFE

Meanwhile, in Damascus, Ananias, a disciple of Christ had a dream, instructing him to look after Paul. But Ananias was afraid, because he knew that Paul had arrested and imprisoned many Christians. So the voice of the Lord said to him, "Go to him, because I have chosen him to be my instrument and to announce the Gospel to all peoples."

Ananias understood that the Lord had changed Paul's heart, and there was nothing to fear from him. Ananias went to find Paul and when he saw him he said, "My brother, Jesus has sent me to you, it was he who appeared to you on the road to Damascus. He has sent me to you, so that you can receive life and the Holy Spirit."

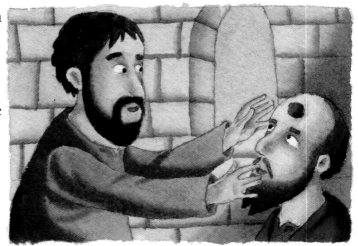

Ananias touched Paul and he could see once more.

Paul was baptised and began a new life. Nothing was ever the same because the meeting with Jesus on the road to Damascus had changed him completely.

As he wrote in his letters, that day, Jesus had "captured" and "imprisoned" him forever. Paul passed some years in solitude in the deserts of Arabia. His heart, that had been full of hatred for Jesus' followers, now felt something new. He had received instruction from Ananias, but his real teacher remained Jesus, who guided his heart, and showed him the greatness and originality of the Christian message.

When Paul returned to Damascus, he began to preach the Gospel, but those who used to be his friends no longer understood him. It seemed to them that he had abandoned the faith of his fathers, and they were shocked, the Pharisees turned against him and forced him to flee.

A MESSAGE FOR EVERYONE

Paul went to Jerusalem and was looked after by Barnabas, a Jew who had accepted Jesus' message. There, he met the apostles Peter and James. Because of what he had done in the past however, Paul could see that people were careful and silent around him.

One day when he was on the way to the temple to pray, Christ appeared to him again and showed him what his mission in the new-born Church would be bringing the Gospel to the pagans. This meant making disciples of every nation, not only among the Jews. The message of Christ, who gave his life for all, was for all, without distinction!

Later in that year, Paul would write, "There is no longer Jew or Greek, or slave or free man, nor male or female, for all are one in Christ Jesus."

Soon Paul had to leave for Tarsus, because the city of Jerusalem had not welcomed him, and he was advised to leave it.

Paul lived in Tarsus, working as a tent maker. He was there for several years, during which his faith in Jesus grew. He felt that Jesus' words had now taken the place that the Law of Moses had once held in his heart. But this did not mean that he forgot the traditions of his fathers. Paul saw that the Law and faith of Israel were meant to teach and prepare them for the coming of Jesus, the Messiah.

Before, salvation was gained by following the Law and doing all that it prescribed, now there was a new Law, a Law that God himself had put into people's hearts. Paul was sure that faith was a gift of the Holy Spirit and the only law to follow was that of loving God and one's neighbour. In one of his letters he said, "Love is the fulfilment of the Law."

THE FIRST MISSIONARY JOURNEY

One day, a man called Barnabas arrived in Tarsus, and asked Paul to follow him to Antioch in Syria; where there was a growing Christian community. There were some non-Jews who wanted to be part of it. Barnabas asked for Paul's help and Paul said yes, he was ready to follow him, convinced that the Gospel had to be preached to the Gentiles, to the pagans.

They worked together for a year, announcing the Good News and looking after the Christian community in Antioch. It was the first place where followers of Christ were called "Christians".

Barnabas and Paul decided to undertake their first missionary journey. They left Antioch and went to Cyprus and then to the southern regions of Turkey. They had many difficulties, but they found that the pagans accepted God's message of love. This encouraged them, even when problems arose with those who thought that to protect Judaism all the non-Jews who entered the community had to observe Jewish practices and traditions. Paul did not agree. Anyone could accept the Christian message without having to live like a Jew.

In the year 49, in order to talk about these problems, a meeting was called in Jerusalem. The meeting would become the first Council in the Church's history. Peter, James, Paul and others all spoke. In the end, they agreed that salvation comes from Jesus and the Holy Spirit, and it is not necessary to make pagans follow the Law of Moses. The apostles also officially recognised Paul's work of announcing God's love to the pagans.

PAUL AND SILAS IN JAIL

From that time, Paul was always travelling, over land and sea, bravely and without a rest. He visited far away cities, teaching people about the Christian faith.

Together with a man called Silas, he arrived in Galatia, then he moved again. When he and Silas got to Philippi, they were arrested and brought into the main square before the elders of the city. They were charged with causing trouble and preaching a very different message to that of the Roman religions that were practiced there.

Paul and Silas were beaten and thrown into prison.

During the night the two woke up to pray. Many of the prisoners watched, when suddenly there was an earthquake that shook the foundations of the prison and opened the door of their cell. The guard was frightened, thinking that they had escaped and he would be blamed, but Paul and Silas remained where they were and said to him, "Don't be afraid, we are here."

The guard then wished to get to know them, and Paul announced the Gospel to him.

During the night, the guard took them to his home and looked after them, making sure their wounds were tended and inviting them to eat with him and his family. Then Paul and Silas returned to their cell, and in the morning the authorities let them go.

Paul was soon back on the road, travelling to Thessalonica, Athens and Corinth, where he stopped and stayed for nearly two years.

In each of these cities, Paul founded a Christian community that he kept in touch with. He continued to write to them when he was far away, letters in which he deepened and explained his teachings, as well as correcting and encouraging them.

ANOTHER MISSION

Paul went back to Antioch, but he did not stay long. He set off again on his third trip. His most important stop this time was in the city of Ephesus. There, Paul set up a centre for learning about the Christian faith, and he met many different people. He had daily meetings where he preached the Gospel.

Many believed and Paul's teachings became well known. But not everyone was happy about this new message. In Ephesus, there were many craftsmen, who made statues and figures of the old gods, and especially of Artemis. They were not pleased because Paul's words encouraged people to leave behind these false religions (which they made a living from) and stop buying their statues.

That meant that these workmen made less money. The silversmiths forced Paul to leave the city and he went into Macedonia again. He stayed three months in Corinth, and escaped a trap that was laid for

him on a ship he was meant to board. Continuing his journey on land, Paul was accompanied by Luke the evangelist, and together they arrived in Jerusalem, bringing money, given in Greece and Macedonia to help the city's Christians.

IN JERUSALEM

In Jerusalem, Paul was overjoyed to see the Christian community. Unfortunately there were still people who had not forgiven him for what he had done when he was young. One day, Paul was accused of taking a non-Jew into the temple in Jerusalem: according to the Law of Moses, this meant profaning the holiest place in the Jewish faith. Paul was arrested, charged and brought before the Sanhedrin. In the end, because of an order of the Roman official Antonius Felix, Paul was sent to Caesarea, where he spent two years in prison.

When, in the year 60, a proper trial was put in place for him at Jerusalem, Paul refused to go, reminding them that he was a Roman citizen and could appeal to the emperor.

So, being escorted by a centurion, Paul and Luke set out for Rome.

The ship that they boarded was hit by a storm and wrecked on the island of Malta, in the centre of the Mediterranean, south of Sicily.

After a month's rest, the survivors began their journey again. They travelled through Sicily and southern Italy, arriving in Rome in the year 61.

ROME

Paul and the others were allowed to live in a barracks watched by guards. There, Paul managed to contact the Christians of Rome and he met and talked with them. He continued to spread the Gospel and wrote letters to the communities he had founded, giving them hope and encouraging them to follow Jesus' example.

We know little about the last years of Paul's life. It is possible he was freed and tried to get to Spain, for he certainly had wanted to get there. It is also probable that he returned to Ephesus. Then, he was once again arrested and brought back to Rome.

In the year 66, Paul was finally condemned to death for being a Christian. It was a difficult moment for the Christians: they were persecuted throughout the Roman Empire, they were arrested and their goods and property confiscated. Unless they denied their faith, by sacrificing to Roman gods, they were killed.

Paul, who years before went looking for Christians to arrest them, preferred to give up his life, rather than give up his faith in Jesus.

He was beheaded, probably in the year 67, this is why he is always shown holding a sword in paintings or statues. He had taken the Gospel to the far corners of the empire, and above all, to its capital, Rome.

In one of his letters we read, "Bless those who persecute you, bless and do not curse. Do not repay evil with evil. Try to do good to all men. Do not let yourself be won over by evil, but overcome evil with good."